William Makepeace Thayer

Lincoln's Boyhood

William Makepeace Thayer

Lincoln's Boyhood

ISBN/EAN: 9783743327238

Manufactured in Europe, USA, Canada, Australia, Japa

Cover: Foto ©ninafisch / pixelio.de

Manufactured and distributed by brebook publishing software (www.brebook.com)

William Makepeace Thayer

Lincoln's Boyhood

CHAPTER I.

BIRTHPLACE.

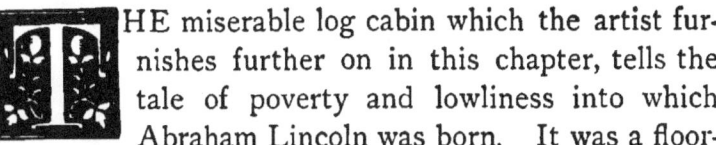HE miserable log cabin which the artist furnishes further on in this chapter, tells the tale of poverty and lowliness into which Abraham Lincoln was born. It was a floorless, doorless, windowless shanty, situated in one of the most barren and desolate spots of Hardin county, Kentucky. His father made it his home simply because he was too poor to own a better one. Nor was his an exceptional case of penury and want. For the people of that section were generally poor and unlettered, barely able to scrape enough together to keep the wolf of hunger from their abodes.

Here Abraham Lincoln was born February 12th, 1809. His father's name was Thomas Lincoln; his mother's maiden name was Nancy Hanks. When they were married, Thomas was twenty-eight years of age, and Nancy, his wife, twenty-three. They had been married three years when Abraham was born. Their cabin was in that part of Hardin County which is now embraced in La Rue County, a few miles from Hodgensville — on the south fork of Nolin Creek. A perennial spring of water, gushing in silvery brightness from beneath a rock near by, relieved the barrenness of the location, and won for it the somewhat ambitious name — " Rock Spring Farm."

" How came Thomas Lincoln here ? " the reader will ask, " Whence did he come ? " " Who were his ancestors ? "

Thomas Lincoln was born in Rockingham County, Virginia, in 1778. Two years later (in 1780), his father lured by the stories of the remarkable fertility of the soil in Kentucky, and the rapid growth of the population, removed thither for a permanent abode. He had five children at the time — three sons and two daughters — and Thomas was the youngest child but one. He settled in Mercer, now Bullitt County.

Then, a hundred years ago, the Indians in that region, and throughout the whole north-west territory, were deadly hostile to the whites. The pioneer "took his life into his hands" by removing thither. His rifle was his constant companion, that he might defend himself against the savage foe, whether at home or abroad. If he went to the field to plough or build fence, or into the woods to chop, his rifle was indispensable. He knew not when or where the wily Indian would surprise him.

Four years after the father of Thomas Lincoln moved into Kentucky, he went into the field to build fence. He took Thomas, who was then about six years old, with him, and sent his two older sons, Mordecai and Josiah, to work in another field not far away. While busily engaged in putting up fence, a party of Indians in ambush fired at the father and he fell dead. The sons were terribly frightened, and little Thomas was well-nigh paralyzed. Josiah ran to a stockade two miles off, and Mordecai, the eldest, ran to the cabin, from the loft of which, through a loop-hole, he could see the Indians. A savage was in the act of lifting his little brother from the ground, whereupon Mordecai, aiming his gun through the hole in the loft, fired, and killed the "redskin." The latter fell to the ground instantly and Thomas ran for his life to the cabin. Mordecai continued at his post, blazing away at the head of every Indian who peered from the underbrush. Soon, however, Josiah arrived from the stockade with a party of settlers; and the savages fled, leaving their dead comrade and a wounded one behind them. Mordecai had done good execution with his rifle.

That was the darkest day that the family of Abraham Lincoln's grandfather ever knew. The lifeless form of their strong protector, borne into their humble cabin, made it desolate indeed. Who would defend them now? To whom would they look for bread? A home in the wilderness was hardship enough, but the fatal shot of the savage multiplied hardships an hundred fold.

Abraham Lincoln often listened, in his boyhood, to this tale of woe in his grandfather's cabin. It was a chapter of family history too startling and important to be passed over with a single rehearsal. It was stereotyped and engraved upon Abraham's young heart, with many other reminiscences and facts connected with life in Kentucky at that early day. His father was a great story-teller, and was noted for his "yarns," and besides, a sort of pride prompted the recital of this exciting chapter of family history, with scenes that preceded it.

"It would take me a week," he would say, "to tell you all I have heard your grandpa say about those dark days. The very year he came here, 1780, the Indians attacked the settlers in great force. All the men were ordered to organize into companies, and Daniel Boone, 'the great hunter of Kentucky,' who settled there five years before the Lincolns did, was made a lieutenant-colonel, and all the forces were put under the charge of General Clark. They started to meet the enemy, and found them near the Lower Blue Licks. Here they fought a terrible battle, and the Indians beat, and cut up the whites badly. Boone's son was wounded, and his father tried to carry him away in the retreat. He plunged into the river with him on his back, but the boy died before he reached the other side. By the time Boone got over the river, he looked around and saw that the Indians were swimming after him; so he had to throw down his dead son, and run for his life. He got away and reached Bryant's Station in safety. Before that, the Indians captured three little girls and carried them off. They belonged to the fort at Boonesboro, and one of them was Boone's daughter. They were playing with a canoe in the Kentucky river, and crossed over to the other side, when a party of Indians rushed out of the bushes into the river and drew the canoe ashore. The girls were scared almost to death, and screamed so loud that they were heard at the fort. The men in the fort ran out to help them, but by the time they reached the canoe, the savages had fled with the girls. It was almost night — too late to organize and pursue them, and so they spent the night in mustering all the men they could and started after them at break of day. But it was well nigh the close of the next day when the settlers came in sight of the Indians, forty miles off. They had camped for the night, and were cooking their supper. Fearing that the Indians would kill the girls rather than give them up, it was the plan of the settlers to shoot them so suddenly that they would have no time to kill the girls. So they banged away at the savages, all of them together, as soon as they came in sight of them, taking good care not to hit the children. Not one shot hit an Indian, but the attack was so sudden and uproarious, that the red-skins were scared half out of their wits; and they ran away as fast as their legs could carry them, leaving the girls and their weapons behind."

Abraham's young life was regaled with many such "yarns"—real facts of history—belonging to the times and experience of his ancestors. Whatever may have been the effect of these "harrowing tales" upon his mind, it is quite certain that he must have seen, by contrast, that his own condition, with all its want and woe, was a decided improvement upon that of his grandfather's family.

But to return to our story, Abraham's grandmother removed after her husband was shot; and Thomas, his father, was compelled to shift for himself as soon as he was old enough to work for his living. Being a rover by nature, and under the necessity of supporting himself, he wandered about from place to place in search of jobs, and took up his abode wherever there was a chance to earn his bread and butter. He was not very enterprising, nor particularly industrious at this period of his life. He loved a roving life too well and was too well satisfied with jolly companions to mean business. His wandering career, however, showed him much of the world, and furnished the opportunity to store his mind with anecdotes and some useful information, which he made frequent use of in after years, and by reason of which, he became very popular with his associates.

When Thomas Lincoln was about twenty-six years of age, he went to live with Joseph Hanks, a carpenter, of Elizabethtown, Kentucky, to learn his trade. It was here that he met Nancy Hanks, niece of Joseph Hanks, whom he courted and afterwards married, thereby getting, not only a trade, but a wife, also. The latter, however, was much more of an acquisition than the former; for he was never competent to do any but the roughest work at his trade. When he was married to Nancy he set up housekeeping in a more miserable abode at Elizabethtown than the log cabin on Nolin Creek. From this shanty, into which he took his bride, he soon removed to the other shanty on the aforesaid Creek.

This is how and why Thomas Lincoln, father of Abraham, became the proprietor of the rickety habitation in Hardin county, that we have described to the reader. Here three children were born to him; Sarah, the eldest, Abraham next, and Thomas the third. The latter died in infancy.

Thomas Lincoln could neither read nor write. He had not been to school a single day in his life. His wife could read passably, but she could not write sufficiently to undertake a letter. She could sign her name to a document, and perhaps do a little more in the same line; while her husband could only make his mark.

"You can learn," said his bride to him, soon after the twain became one flesh. "Never too old to learn."

"That's a question," responded her husband, who was one of the easy bodies, who could scarcely think it worth while for a man to go to school, even to his wife, at twenty-eight years of age.

"It's not a question at all," responded Mrs. L. "You can learn to write your name, if nothing more, and that will be a great improvement over making your mark. I can teach you as much as that."

At length the good-natured husband consented to take lessons of his wife in penmanship; and he actually set to work to accomplish his purpose. The most that he accomplished, however, was to learn to write his name so that ingenious people could read it. He lifted himself out of that ignorant and unambitious class who are content to make their ×.

At this time Thomas Lincoln and his wife were members of the Baptist Church, showing that they cast in their lot with the best people of the county, and aspired to a Christian life. Mrs. Lincoln was a more devout follower of Christ than her husband, and was more gifted mentally. Dr. Holland says: "She was a slender, pale, sad, and sensitive woman, with much in her nature that was truly heroic, and much that shrank from the rude life around her." Lamon says: "By her family her understanding was considered something wonderful." There is no doubt that she was a bright, sensible, brave Christian woman, whose father removed from Virginia into Kentucky about the time that the father of Thomas Lincoln did. Thomas appears to have been satisfied with his choice, and her influence over him was strong and elevating.

When Abraham was four years old, his father removed to a more fertile and picturesque spot on Knob Creek, six miles from Hodgensville. This creek empties into the Rolling Fork, the Rolling Fork into Salt River, and Salt River into the Ohio, twenty-four miles from Louisville. How so poor a man could purchase so much of a farm (two hundred and thirty-eight acres) for one hundred and eighteen pounds, seems mysterious, until we learn the fact that, at the end of the year, he sold two hundred acres for one hundred pounds, reserving but thirty-eight acres for himself. But even this condition of his affairs shows a decided advance in contrast with the pitiable poverty that inducted him into wedded life. Then, too, the fact that he aspired after a more fertile and attractive location, and actually planted from six to eight acres the first year of his residence on Knob Creek, proves that the spirit of a larger enterprise possessed his soul. Somehow his marriage to Nancy Hanks had raised him above that restless, thriftless, aimless life that characterized his youth and early manhood.

It was on Knob Creek that Abraham, or "Abe," as he was familiarly called by his parents and other people, was initiated into fishing and other sports. On Nolin Creek he hunted "ground-hogs" with a precocious boy, Johnnie Duncan, who afterwards became quite widely known as Rev. John Duncan. On Knob Creek, he played in the water, took long tramps, and enjoyed himself generally with one Billy Gallaher. For a boy of his age (but six or seven at that time) he was adventurous and enterprising. One of his venturesome sports was, to catch hold of a branch of a sycamore tree and swing over the water. One day, when indulging in this risky sport, with his no less venturesome Billy, he lost his hold of the limb and plunged into the water. If Billy had not been a cool, smart, efficient boy, Thomas Lincoln would have lost a good son on that day, and the United States of America a good President. But Billy was equal to the occasion, and, by brave efforts, succeeded in delivering "Abe" from a watery grave.

Another boy, Dennis F. Hanks, his cousin, was one of his boon companions, though a little older than himself. Thomas Sparrow, who reared Nancy Hanks to womanhood (Mrs. Lincoln), had given Dennis a home in his family, and Sparrow was now a neighbor of Thomas Lincoln, and Dennis and "Abe" playmates. Dennis was a great lover of hunting and fishing, and "Abe" accompanied him upon many a long tramp, though he was not old enough to use fire-arms; nor did he ever become expert in either hunting or fishing.

The Lincoln cabin on Knob Creek was very little better than the one on Nolin Creek. It was a floorless log-house, with one room below and a loft above, and the usual accompaniment of stools, skillet, and Dutch oven. Here "Abe" began to show signs of remarkable brightness, as evinced by his tact, intelligence and aims. It was noticeable that he was more precocious than other children of his age; and his parents were not slow to perceive and appreciate the fact. The next chapter presents him in a new *rôle*.

CHAPTER II.

A SCHOOLBOY.

"BINEY is going to keep school," remarked Mr. Lincoln to his wife, one day, "and he wants to know if Sarah and Abe will go."

"I hope so, certainly, though *he* can't be much of a teacher any way," replied Mrs. Lincoln. "A poor school is better than none."

"There can be no doubt about that," continued Mr. Lincoln. "It won't take Riney long to tell the children all he knows; but that is better than nothing."

"He can't write nor cipher," added his wife, "and a man who can't do that can't be much of a reader."

"Well, reading is all he claims," said Mr. Lincoln. "He has nothing to do with figures or writing. He proposes to teach boys and girls what he knows, and nothing more."

"That's about all the best of them can do, — teach what they know," — Mrs. Lincoln answered. "To attempt more would be foolish indeed."

This Hezekiah Riney was a new comer, and he had settled within a half mile of Lincoln's cabin. He was a rough, ignorant man, with scarcely one qualification for a teacher, even in that wild untutored country.

But he wanted to eke out a miserable subsistence by adding a few dollars to his pitiable income ; and so he proposed school-keeping as about the only thing possible in that barren country. Parents accepted the proposition because there was nothing better ; and here the hero of this volume began to be a schoolboy, accompanying his sister Sarah daily to Riney's cabin. "Abe" made some progress at this school — he began to read. A dilapidated copy of Dillworth's spelling-book was the only volume the two children of Tom Lincoln had between them at this Riney institution, and they appear to have made good use of it. The brightness of the pupils was a pleasant offset to the stupidity of the teacher.

Riney's school, for some reason, was of short duration ; it closed in five or six weeks. Perhaps the fountain ran dry in that time. Possibly some of the scholars knew more than their master at the end of that period, which is not claiming very much for the pupils. At any rate, "Abe" and his sister transferred their destiny to another "pioneer college," as, forty years afterwards, Abraham Lincoln facetiously called those cabin-schools of the woods.

"Mr. Hazel knows a heap more than Riney," said Mr. Lincoln, "and we must try to have the children go to his school, though it is a long way off."

"Yes; it is time that 'Abe knew something about writing,' and Hazel can learn him that," Mrs. L. replied. "The children won't mind the distance. If we can scrape together enough to pay for their schooling, they ought to go."

The last remark touched upon a subject that was

often uppermost in Tom Lincoln's mind,— how to get money enough to pay for the necessaries of life. Although he was satisfied with corn-cake and milk for daily food, yet it would require considerable ingenuity and economy to produce the extra money to pay for the schooling ; so he replied,—

"I've counted the cost, and I guess we can raise the money some way. Hazel can start Abe off on writing, and that will be worth everything to him. Some day I hope to live in a country where I can earn something at my trade."

"That will be some distance from here, I'm thinking," replied Mrs. L. "We can't expect much growth in this part of the country at present. If Indiana comes into the Union a free State, there may be a better chance there." The question of admitting Indiana into the Union as a free State was then agitating the country. The subject was before the American Congress, and the slave power was doing every thing possible to prevent such an event. The slaveholders of Kentucky were especially exercised about it, because another free State so near would be an additional invitation to their slaves to find an asylum there. The subject was discussed, pro and con, in every Kentucky cabin where white men dwelt. The Lincolns were in favor of making Indiana a free State. They knew full well that the curse of slavery blighted the prosperity of every slave State.

"There's a better chance for every thing in a free State," was Mr. Lincoln's only answer.

The reader must understand that schools were very scarce in Kentucky in Tom Lincoln's day; and the few in existence were very poor, scarcely deserving the name of schools. They would not be tolerated now. Teachers were no better than the schools; for it is always true, "like teachers, like schools." Hazel's school was better than Riney's; for Hazel could give instruction in "reading and writing." True, his acquisitions in these several branches were small indeed: they compared well with his surroundings. But he could give such a boy as Abraham a start in the right direction.

Hazel's school was four miles distant; and it was kept in a log schoolhouse, the only one in all that region. To this pioneer institution Sarah and Abraham travelled daily, carrying their dinner of corn-bread, without varying it a single day during the eight or ten weeks of their attendance. Here Abraham really began his career. Here he acquired the art of penmanship, very imperfectly, of course; but he learned to form letters, and became enthusiastic over the acquirement. Here, too, he made rapid progress in reading. Mr. Hazel discovered the elements of a noble character in the boy, and predicted that he would not always live in the woods as his father had. The best evidence we can find proves that Abraham learned about all Hazel was able to teach in the few weeks he was his pupil.

All the books the Lincoln cabin could boast, at that time, were the Bible, Catechism, and the copy of Dillworth's Spelling-Book, that Sarah and Abraham shared between them. This was a very small library even for a pioneer, but it was good as far as it went. Any library that begins with the Bible begins well. The

Catechism and Spelling-Book were suitable companions for the Book of books. "The three safeguards of our country are the Bible, Sabbath, and Public School;" and here they were in the Lincoln cabin,—elements of family and national growth. Other things of like value followed in due time.

The religious advantages of that day and region were smaller, if possible, than the educational. There was no worship, nor place of worship, within many miles. "Parson Elkins" embraced that part of Kentucky in his circuit, so that occasionally he preached in the Lincoln cabin, where he was a favorite. Indeed, he was a favorite in all that region, and was cordially welcomed by all settlers who had any respect for religion. With this exception, public worship was unknown among the pioneers of that time, and Christian families were obliged to depend upon themselves chiefly for Bible study and Sabbath observance. As Mrs. Lincoln could read, and the Bible was the only reading-book in the family, Abraham often heard it read upon the Sabbath, and other days. Before he learned to read, he became familiar with many of the narratives of the Bible. He delighted in Bible stories in his childhood, and never tired of listening to their rehearsal. As soon as he could read, the Bible became his reading book, in the absence of all others. Over and over again its narrative portions especially were read, until his mind became stored with Scriptural knowledge. As he grew older, and other reading-books occupied his attention, he neglected the Bible for them. Still, his familiarity with it in his childhood made an impression for life. Though he was not a Christian man when he entered upon his public career, yet he evinced a remarkable familiarity with the Scriptures. His conversation and public addresses were often enlivened by quotations and figures from the Bible. In the sequel it will appear that this one book must have been the source of that honesty, noble ambition, adherence to right, and dependence upon Providence, which signalized his public career.

Three incidents of his life in the White House show his familiarity with the Bible. At one time he was very much annoyed by men who complained of prominent officials. To one of these parties, he said, one day, "Go home, my friend, and read attentively the tenth verse of the thirteenth chapter of Proverbs." That verse is, "Accuse not a servant to his master, lest he curse thee, and thou be found guilty." General Fremont, whom he had relieved of his command, consented to run against him for the Presidency, after Lincoln's renomination for the office. A small following of disappointed politicians and military aspirants rallied around Fremont. About the time the latter withdrew his name,—satisfied that his candidacy would make more enemies than friends,—Mr. Lincoln said to a public man, who introduced the subject, "Look here; hear this;" and he proceeded to read the following from the First Book of Samuel, "And every one that was in distress, and every one that was in debt, and every one that was discontented, gathered themselves unto him, and he became captain over them, and there were with him about four hundred men."

At one time Henry Ward Beecher criticized his administration sharply in the "Independent," of which he was the editor-in-chief. Several editorials of this character were published in that journal, and some one cut them out and forwarded them to Mr. Lincoln. One day he took them out of the envelope and read them all through, when he flung them upon the floor, exclaiming, "Is thy servant a *dog* that he should do this thing?" The criticisms were based on falsehoods, and were therefore unjust and cruel; hence his apt quotation from the Bible.

It has been said by one of Abraham Lincoln's biographers, that his father had no interest in his education. The facts already cited prove such a conclusion to be incorrect. A father and mother whose poverty compelled them to live upon "hoe-cake," must have had a decided interest in the education of their children, to try to scrape together a few dollars for their tuition at school, and then send them four miles on foot daily to enjoy the coveted boon! If that be indifference to culture, then the more we have of it the better. That Thomas Lincoln and his pious wife cherished a strong desire for the education of their children, there can be no doubt; that they saw in their son, Abraham, early evidence of remarkable mental powers is certain; but that they expected he would ever become distinguished as a public man is not true; for there was no prospect whatever that he would lift the incubus of want and obscurity, and step out into the world of renown. Such an anticipation could not possibly have been indulged by them.

. . . .

It was the autumn of 1816. Indiana had been admitted as a free State into the Union, and immigration thither had already set in as a consequence. The excitement over freedom in Indiana had reached Kentucky, as we have said already, and Thomas Lincoln and wife became interested parties. They discussed the question of removing thither, and finally decided in the affirmative, provided their farm could be sold.

"As soon as the fall work is through," was Mr. Lincoln's decision.

"*If* you can sell," added Mrs. L., with a significant emphasis upon the *if*. "It's a hard place to sell anything here. Perhaps we shall have to stay a while longer."

"There'll be somebody to buy," added Mr. L., with a confident air.

"Heard anything from the man Gallaher told about?"

"Not a word; but there's time enough yet."

Neighbor Gallaher had met a person who desired to purchase a small farm like Lincoln's, and he had told him of Lincoln's desire to sell in October, "after the fall work was through." The man's name was Colby; and Mr. Lincoln really expected the would-be purchaser would make his appearance. His wife had little faith in the enterprise, although she really desired to remove to Indiana. The difficulty of selling a farm at such a time and in such a place appeared far greater to her than to her husband.

"We must go soon or not at all this year," added Mrs. L. "Winter will overtake us in the wilderness before we are ready for it."

"It will not take long to pull up stakes and locate in Indiana when we once get started," responded Mr. Lincoln.

"Perhaps not; but it will be time enough to think of that after we sell," suggested his wife, as if she had little faith that a purchaser of their farm could be found. "We must learn to labor and wait."

"We've got that lesson pretty well learned now," responded Mr. Lincoln. "About all I've ever done is to labor and wait; and if I wait much longer I may lose what title I have to my land now, as others have."

"That is not impossible, as everybody about here knows," added Mrs. Lincoln.

"The chances are that the title to this place may prove worthless, judging from the experience of others," continued Mr. Lincoln. "A man don't know whether he owns an acre of land or not about here."

Great excitement prevailed in Kentucky relative to land-titles. Many settlers, after toiling for years for a livelihood, found their titles to their farms defective. The heirs of Daniel Boone were cheated out of every acre of land purchased by their illustrious ancestor. So many had experienced trouble and heavy losses in this way, that almost every landholder feared his title might prove invalid. Thomas Lincoln shared this fear in common with others. One of his biographers maintains that he removed to Indiana solely on this account; — that the curse of slavery in Kentucky, or the advantages of freedom in the new State of Indiana, had nothing to do with his decision. But we beg leave to dissent from this conclusion. There can be no doubt that the uncertainty of land-titles in Kentucky was one important reason for his removal, but it was by no means the only reason. Another reason, without doubt, was his love of change. His roving disposition was not entirely eradicated. But, more than all, the excitement over the making of another free State, with the rose-colored views promulgated concerning the advantages of a free State to poor men like himself, influenced him to make the change. It is positive that he would not have removed to Indiana at all had it come into the Union as a Slave State. The general enthusiasm over its admission in the interest of freedom, lured him thither as it did hundreds of others. The very rapid immigration to that State, commencing immediately after its admission, is conclusive proof of this statement. The reason of his locating just where he did in Indiana was, probably, because a former acquaintance — Thomas Carter — had removed thither. But the next chapter will disclose the details of this affair.

CHAPTER III.

THE OLD HOME SOLD.

ABOUT the middle of October (1816) a stranger appeared at the cabin. It was Colby.

"You want to sell your place, I hear," he remarked, after introducing himself.

"I'm thinking of it," answered Mr. Lincoln. "Gallaher told me that you would come to see me about it. So we've been expecting you, and rather making arrangements to sell the farm. This is about what you would like?"

"Yes, from Mr. Gallaher's description of it. I can't handle much of a place; I'm too poor for that."

"In the same boat with the rest of us, then," suggested Mr. Lincoln. "Not much money in these diggings. How much money can you put into a place?"

"Not much, just now. I must make a barter trade if I buy now. What's the damage for such a place as this?"

"Three hundred dollars," answered Mr. Lincoln promptly. "That is the price I've settled on."

"Cash?"

"Yes; that's what I've been expecting, though I might take something else for part of the pay."

"Well, I haven't much money," continued Mr. Colby; "but I have what is good as money in the market."

"What is it?"

"You see I've been specilatin' a little since I gave you a call in the summer. I used up my grain for whiskey, and I bought some, too, thinkin' that I should make a spec out of it; but I hain't sold but a trifle on't yet. Now, if I could pay you mostly in whiskey, I would strike the bargain at once; and may be that over in Indiana you'll find a ready market for it."

"I hadn't thought of taking pay in such an article," answered Mr. Lincoln; "and I don't know as I could ever sell it. I'm going to strike right into the wilderness."

"That may be; but you'll have neighbors within a few miles; and over there they hain't got the knack of manifacturin' it, I s'pose, and this would make it easier to sell it."

"It's awkward stuff to carry on such a trip, though I expect to move on a flat-boat."

"Just the easiest thing in the world to carry this; you can carry it as well as not on a boat. You won't have half a load of other stuff. And it will bring you double there what it will here, I'm thinkin'."

"That's all guess-work."

"But don't it stand to reason that whiskey would bring more where they can't make it, as they can here?"

"Yes, I admit that it may probably bring more there, and it ought to bring more to pay for the trouble of taking it there. But can't you turn it into money some way?"

"I don't see how I can; I've done the best I could about it. The fact is, the folks in this part of Kentucky have laid in largely for whiskey. I can sell it in time, I have no doubt, at a stiff price, but that won't help me just now."

"Of course not; but this is unexpected, though I'm determined to sell out at some rate. You look over the place; it's all in a stone's throw, and I will talk with my wife, and see what we can do."

So Lincoln left Colby to examine the premises, after having shown him the limits of the place, and proceeded to consult his wife. Mrs. Lincoln looked surprised and amused over the proposition to turn the farm into whiskey. "A queer bargain," she said. "Something I never dreamed of."

"Nor I; but I must sell the place, and this may be my last chance this season."

"That is very true, and the matter must be looked at carefully. It may be that the whiskey can be sold in Indiana more readily than we expect. I scarcely know what to say. You must do as you think best."

"Well, I think it is best to sell out at some rate, and if I thought that this was my last chance to sell this fall, I should take the whiskey, and run the risk."

"As to that, I think it likely that you won't have another chance this fall. It isn't often that you can sell a place in this part of the country."

"I'm inclined to think, then," continued Mr. Lincoln, musing, with his eyes fastened upon the earth-floor of their cabin, as if scarcely knowing what to do, "that I shall take the whiskey if I can't do any better with him."

"Just as you think best," answered his wife. "You can judge better than I can whether it will do or not."

After going to the man, and satisfying himself that he must take the whiskey, or fail to sell, Mr. Lincoln introduced the subject of the price of it, about which nothing had been said.

"How much a gallon?" he inquired. "You'll of course sell it at a discount, seeing I take such a quantity."

"Certainly; I shall sell it to you for five cents a gallon less than the wholesale price of a barrel; and you can't ask anything better than that."

"That's fair, I think ; and now let me see, how much will it take?" The reader must remember that Mr. Lincoln never studied arithmetic, though he could solve such a problem as this, only give him time. He had been obliged to think and act for himself from boyhood, and, of course, contact with men and things had given him some knowledge of figures, or, at least, the ability to perform some problems mentally.

Mr. Lincoln continued: "Seventy cents a gallon — that will be — let me see — seventy cents a gallon — that will — "

"Why, one hundred gallons would come to seventy dollars," interrupted Colby, "and four hundred would come to two hundred and eighty dollars."

"Yes, I see it — four hundred gallons, and the rest in money."

"That is it; it will make just ten barrels of forty gallons each, and twenty dollars in money."

"I see it. I will agree to that. Ten barrels, and

the balance in money. And when shall we close the bargain?"

"Just as soon as you propose to leave."

"That will be about the first of November. I shall want the whiskey and money, though, a week before that, so as to be all ready to start."

"A week before that it is, then. I agree to that, and shall be here promptly at the time. Perhaps I shall bring the whiskey before that, if it comes right."

"Just as well, — as soon as you please."

So the bargain was struck, and Colby left.

Let the reader stop here to ponder this trade. A homestead sold for ten barrels of whiskey and about twenty dollars in money! Surely Abraham's father could not boast much of this world's goods! And then what an article to take in exchange for a homestead! What a prospect for his son! Many a homestead is now bartered away for whiskey, or some other intoxicating beverage, and haggard want is all that remains. But not so in this case. Mr. Lincoln did not countenance immoderate drinking. He used whiskey to some extent, in common with everybody else, but he frowned upon intemperance.

Such a transaction as the above was not thought singular at that day. Good people sold and drank whiskey. There was no temperance movement in Kentucky at that time. Indeed, it was not until about that time that the subject of temperance attracted attention in New England, and then it did not assume the form of total abstinence. The pledge required persons to abstain from immoderate drinking. It was not till fifteen years thereafter that the pledge of total abstinence was adopted.

At the present day the sale of a place for whiskey would excite surprise and amazement, and subject the character of the recipient of the whiskey to suspicion, at least. People would make remarks about it, and strongly suspect that the man loved whiskey more than real estate. But not so at that time, when the sale and use of it was regarded as right and proper in every part of the country.

It was necessary to hasten preparations for removal, as Colby desired to take possession as soon as he could. Mr. Lincoln must take his goods to Indiana by flat-boat, and return for his family, which would require time as well as despatch. He had no flat-boat, and, therefore, was under the necessity of building one. This would require several days of hard labor. He was competent for such an emergency; for he had constructed and run a flat-boat, on one or two trips, to New Orleans, in the company and employment of Isaac Bush. His trade and experience served him a good purpose now.

. . . . .

Arrangements were completed for the flat-boat trip. Colby had arrived with the whiskey and made a settlement with Lincoln; and the singular cargo was loaded. The heavy wares, like his carpenter's tools, pots, kettles, stools, puncheon-table, axes, etc., were loaded upon the boat with the whiskey; and the many other things necessary to be done before "pulling up stakes," as Lincoln called it, were attended to.

Mrs. Lincoln, Sarah, and Abraham, who had watched

the progress of the boat-building with peculiar interest, and seen the boat launched and loaded, waited upon the bank as the homely craft was pushed out into deep water and floated down the river.

We cannot stop to detail much that occurred on the voyage. One incident, however, deserves attention.

He had floated down the Rolling Fork into the Ohio River, and proceeded quite a distance on his voyage, experiencing no perils of wind or storm; and he was congratulating himself upon his success, when he met with an accident. By some mishap, the boat tilted, and the whiskey rolled from its position to the side, causing him to upset. He sprung forward to the other side in order to save his boat, but it was too late. The whiskey was heavy, and, once started from its position, there was no saving it or the boat. In a moment he was tipped into the water, with all his cargo. It was a good place for the whiskey, but not so pleasant for him. However, he clung to the boat, and made the best of it.

"Hold on there!" shouted a man who was at work with three others on the bank of the river. "Hold on, and we'll come to your help." He was not more than three rods from the bank.

"Quick as you can," replied Mr. Lincoln.

"We'll be there in a jiffy," bawled one of them, and all ran for a boat that was tied about twenty rods below.

One of the number leaped into it, and, plying the oar with all his might, he soon reached the craft that was upset, and took Mr. Lincoln on board.

"Bad business for you," said the man.

"Not so bad as it might be," answered Mr. Lincoln. "Rather lucky, I think, to meet with such an accident where help is close by."

"But you've lost your cargo, though we may save some of it if we set about it."

"Won't save much of it, I'm thinking. The water is ten or fifteen feet deep there."

"Hardly that."

"Pretty near it, I'll warrant."

By this time they had reached the bank of the river, and the men were consulting together about righting Lincoln's boat and saving his cargo. Such accidents were not uncommon on the Ohio, and those who lived along the bank had lent a helping hand to many unfortunate adventurers. This was the case with the men who came to Lincoln's rescue. They were not long in laying their plans, nor dilatory in executing them.

In a short time they secured his boat, and succeeded in putting it in good trim. They proceeded, also, to save so much of his cargo as they could. They called other men in the neighborhood, and, with such apparatus as the vicinity afforded, they raked the river, and recovered a part of his carpenters' tools, axes, a spider, and some other articles. By much perseverance and hard labor they succeeded in saving three barrels of the whiskey. All these articles were reloaded upon Lincoln's boat, and, with many thanks to the kind-hearted men for their assistance, he proceeded on his way.

Before starting again, however, he consulted the men who aided him with regard to the future of his way; and he decided, in view of the information derived from them, to land at Thompson's Ferry, and there secure a team to convey his goods into the interior. He had previously settled in his mind, as we have said, what part of Indiana he should make his home.

Accordingly he took his boat and goods to Thompson's Ferry, and there he found a man by the name of Posey, whom he hired to take him eighteen miles, into what is now Spencer County. This Posey owned a yoke of oxen, and was quite well acquainted with that section of country.

"No road into that county," said he. "We shall have to pick our way, and use the ax some at that."

"I am sorry for that," answered Lincoln. "Are there no settlers in that region?"

"Yes; here and there one, and they'll be right glad to see you. We can put it through, if you say so."

"Put it through, then, I say," replied Lincoln.

The man agreed to carry his goods to his place of destination, and take his boat for pay. Lincoln would have no further use for his boat, so that it was a good bargain for him, and equally good for Posey, who wanted a boat.

Accordingly, the team was loaded with his effects, and they were soon on their way. But, within a few miles, they were obliged to use the ax to make a road.

"Just as I expected," said Posey. "I have been through the mill."

"How far do you expect we shall have to cut through places like this?" inquired Lincoln.

"Far enough, I have no doubt; this is a real wilderness."

"Then, we must go at it, if we'd see the end soon."

"Yes; and hard work, too, it will be." And, without wasting time or breath on words, they proceeded to cut a road before them.

"I've cut through miles of just such a wilderness as this," said Posey; "and I shouldn't be surprised if we had to cut a road half the way."

"I hope not," answered Lincoln. "If I thought so, I should almost wish myself back in Kentucky."

"Should, hey?"

"Yes; it would be an everlasting job to cut through to where I am going."

"Well, I don't suppose it will be as tough as this much of the way, but bad enough, no doubt."

So with the resolution of veteran pioneers they toiled on, sometimes being able to pick their way for a long distance without chopping, and then coming to a stand-still in consequence of dense forests. Suffice to say, that they were obliged to cut a road so much of the way that several days were employed in going eighteen miles. It was a difficult, wearisome, trying journey, and Mr. Lincoln often said that he never passed through a harder experience than he did in going from Thompson's Ferry to Spencer County, Indiana.

Some two or three miles south of their place of destination they passed the cabin of a hospitable settler, who gave them a hearty welcome, and such refreshments as his humble abode contained. He was well acquainted with all that region, too, and suggested to

Mr. Lincoln the spot upon which he decided to erect his cabin, and also volunteered to accompany them thither.

The settlers at that day delighted to see others coming to their vicinity to dwell, thus increasing their neighbors, and removing somewhat the loneliness of pioneer life. They were ever ready to lend a helping-hand to new-comers, and to share with them the scanty blessings that Providence allowed them.

Mr. Lincoln was glad to reach the end of his journey; and he found the spot suggested by his new friend in the cabin, whose name was Wood, a very inviting one.

"Better than I expected," said Lincoln. "I wouldn't ask for a better place than this."

"I've had my eye on it some time," replied Wood.

"Chance for more settlers, though," continued Lincoln. "One cabin in eighteen miles ain't very thick."

"That's so," added Posey. "There's elbow-room for a few more families, and it won't be long before they'll be here."

"But you've neighbors nearer than that," said Wood. "There's one family not more than two miles east of here."

"Then I shall have two neighbors," said Lincoln.

"And there are two other families within six or eight miles,—one of them is north, and the other west," continued Wood. "The fact is, people are flockin' into this free State fast."

We must not dwell. Posey returned with his team to Thompson's Ferry, and Mr. Lincoln, having deposited his goods, and secured Mr. Wood's promise to

"Far enough, I have no doubt; this is a real wilderness."

"Then, we must go at it, if we'd see the end soon."

"Yes; and hard work, too, it will be." And, without wasting time or breath on words, they proceeded to cut a road before them.

"I've cut through miles of just such a wilderness as this," said Posey; "and I shouldn't be surprised if we had to cut a road half the way."

"I hope not," answered Lincoln. "If I thought so, I should almost wish myself back in Kentucky."

"Should, hey?"

"Yes; it would be an everlasting job to cut through to where I am going."

"Well, I don't suppose it will be as tough as this much of the way, but bad enough, no doubt."

So with the resolution of veteran pioneers they toiled on, sometimes being able to pick their way for a long distance without chopping, and then coming to a stand-still in consequence of dense forests. Suffice to say, that they were obliged to cut a road so much of the way that several days were employed in going eighteen miles. It was a difficult, wearisome, trying journey, and Mr. Lincoln often said that he never passed through a harder experience than he did in going from Thompson's Ferry to Spencer County, Indiana.

Some two or three miles south of their place of destination they passed the cabin of a hospitable settler, who gave them a hearty welcome, and such refreshments as his humble abode contained. He was well acquainted with all that region, too, and suggested to

Mr. Lincoln the spot upon which he decided to erect his cabin, and also volunteered to accompany them thither.

The settlers at that day delighted to see others coming to their vicinity to dwell, thus increasing their neighbors, and removing somewhat the loneliness of pioneer life. They were ever ready to lend a helping-hand to new-comers, and to share with them the scanty blessings that Providence allowed them.

Mr. Lincoln was glad to reach the end of his journey; and he found the spot suggested by his new friend in the cabin, whose name was Wood, a very inviting one.

"Better than I expected," said Lincoln. "I wouldn't ask for a better place than this."

"I've had my eye on it some time," replied Wood.

"Chance for more settlers, though," continued Lincoln. "One cabin in eighteen miles ain't very thick."

"That's so," added Posey. "There's elbow-room for a few more families, and it won't be long before they'll be here."

"But you've neighbors nearer than that," said Wood. "There's one family not more than two miles east of here."

"Then I shall have two neighbors," said Lincoln.

"And there are two other families within six or eight miles,—one of them is north, and the other west," continued Wood. "The fact is, people are flockin' into this free State fast."

We must not dwell. Posey returned with his team to Thompson's Ferry, and Mr. Lincoln, having deposited his goods, and secured Mr. Wood's promise to look after them, directed his steps on foot back to his family. It was about one hundred miles from his old home in Kentucky to his new one in Indiana. This was the distance, in a direct line. It was twenty-five miles further, the way Mr. Lincoln came. It was a part of his plan to return on foot. A direct line, about southeast, would bring him to Hardin County, — a three days' journey.

His family gave him a cordial welcome, and Abraham was somewhat taken with the story of his father's adventure, particularly the part relating to his plunge into the Ohio River.

Hasty preparations were made to remove the family, and such things as he did not take with him on the boat. He took no bedding or apparel with him on the boat. These were left to go with the family, on horseback. Two horses were provided, and on these were packed the aforesaid articles, — Mrs. Lincoln, her daughter, and Abraham sometimes riding and sometimes walking.

They were seven days in performing the journey, camping out nights, with no other shelter than the starry skies over them, and no other bed than blankets spread upon the ground.

It was a novel experience even to them, nor was it without its perils. Yet they had no fears. In that country, at that day, neither men nor women allowed themselves to cower in the presence of dangers.

Females were not the timid class that they are now. They were distinguished for heroism that was truly wonderful. Inured as they were to hardships and perils, they learned to look dangers steadily in the face, and to consider great privations as incidental to pioneer life. Experiences that would now destroy the happiness of most of the sex then served to develop the courage and other intrepid virtues that qualified them for the mission God designed they should fulfil.

Many facts are found in history illustrating the heroism of Western females in the early settlement of that part of our country. Soon after Abraham's grandfather removed to Kentucky, an Indian entered the cabin of a Mr. Daviess, armed with gun and tomahawk, for the purpose of plundering it, and capturing the family. Mrs. Daviess was alone with her children. With remarkable presence of mind she invited the Indian to drink, at the same time setting a bottle of whiskey on the table. The Indian set down his gun to pour out a dram, and at once Mrs. Daviess seized it, and, aiming it at his head, threatened to blow his brains out if he did not surrender. The Indian dropped the bottle, sat down upon a stool, and promised to do no harm if she would not fire. In that position she kept him until her husband arrived.

In another instance, about the same time, the house of a Mr. Merrill was attacked in the night by several Indians, and Mr. Merrill was seriously wounded as he went to the door. The savages attempted to enter the house, when Mrs. Merrill and her daughter shut the door against them, and held it. Then the Indians hewed away a part of the door, so that one of them could get in at a time. But Mrs. Merrill, though her husband lay groaning and weltering in his blood, and her children were screaming with fright, seized an ax, when the first one had got partly into the room, and dealt upon him a mortal blow. Then she drew his body in and waited for the approach of another. The Indians, supposing that their comrade had forced an entrance, were exultant, and proceeded to follow him. Nor did they discover their mistake until she had despatched four of them in this way. Then two of them attempted to descend the chimney, whereupon she ordered her children to empty the contents of a bed upon the fire; and the fire and smoke soon brought down two Indians, half suffocated, into the room. Mr. Merrill, by a desperate exertion, rose up, and speedily finished these two with a billet of wood. At the same time his wife dealt so heavy a blow upon the only remaining Indian at the door, that he was glad to retire.

Volumes might be filled with stories that show the heroism of Western women at that day. We have cited these two examples simply to exhibit their fortitude. Mrs. Lincoln was a resolute, fearless woman, like her pioneer sisters, and hence was cool and self-possessed amidst all exposures and dangers.

We said they were seven days on the journey. Two miles from their destination they came to the cabin of their nearest neighbor, Mr. Neale, who treated them with great kindness, and promised to assist them on the following day in putting up a dwelling. It was a pleasant proffer of assistance, and it served to make them happier as they lay down in their blankets on the first night of their residence in Spencer County, Indiana.

We have been thus particular, in this part of the narrative, because this experience had much to do with the development of that courage, energy, decision, and perseverance for which Abraham was thereafter distinguished.

CHAPTER IV.

A NEW HOME MADE.

IT was in the new home in Indiana that Abraham began to be a genuine pioneer boy. The ax was the symbol of pioneer life; and here he began to swing one in dead earnest. From the time he was eight years old until he had past his majority, he was accustomed to the almost daily use of the ax. His physical strength developed with wonderful rapidity, so that he became one of the most efficient wood-choppers in that region. After he became President, and the "War of the Rebellion" was on his hands, he visited the hospitals at City Point, where three thousand sick and wounded soldiers were sheltered. He insisted upon shaking hands with every one of them; and, after performing the feat, and friends were expressing their fears that his arm would be lamed by so much hand-shaking, he remarked, — "The hardships of my early life gave me strong muscles." And, stepping out of the open door, he took up a very large, heavy ax which lay there by a log of wood, and chopped vigorously for a few moments, sending the chips flying in all directions; and, then pausing, he extended his right arm to its full length, holding the ax out horizontally, without its even quivering as he held it. Strong men who looked on—men accustomed to manual labor—could not hold the same ax in that position for a moment. When the President left, a hospital steward gathered up the chips, and laid them aside carefully, "because they were the chips that Father Abraham chopped."

It was necessary for the Lincoln family to erect a habitation as soon as possible, and "a half-faced camp" could be more easily and quickly built than a cabin, because it could be constructed of "poles" instead of logs. For this reason, Mr. Lincoln decided to erect the "camp" for a temporary abode, and the next year build a substantial log-cabin. He could cut the logs and prepare slabs during the winter, so that the labor of erecting a cabin would not be great after the planting of the next spring was done.

A "half-faced camp" was "a cabin enclosed on three sides and open on the fourth," a very poor habitation for the cold winters of Indiana. But pioneers accepted almost any device for a shelter, and made the best of cold, hunger, and hardship.

Abraham began pioneer life by assisting his father in erecting the "camp." Cutting "poles" was an easy method of initiating him into the hard work of chopping wood. It was not, however, until the following summer when the more substantial cabin was erected, that Abraham engaged in the enterprise with all his heart. A severe winter and unusual exposure caused him to appreciate a better habitation.

After "clearing some land, and planting corn and vegetables," in the spring of 1817, and the summer work was well under way, Mr. Lincoln proceeded to erect his log-cabin. His nearest neighbor rendered him essential aid, and Abraham proved himself very efficient for a boy of eight years. One who often found shelter under the hospitable roof of this cabin has furnished the following description of it: —

"It was sixteen by eighteen feet in size, without a floor, the unhewn logs put together at the corners by the usual method of notching them, and the cracks between them stopped with clay. It had a shed-roof, covered with slabs or clapboards split from logs. It contained but one room, with a loft, slabs being laid on the logs overhead, so as to make a chamber, to which access was had by pins driven into the logs in one corner. It had one door and one window. The latter, however, was so ingeniously constructed, that it deserves particular attention. Mr. Lincoln made a sash of the size of four six-by-eight squares of glass; and, in place of glass, which could not be obtained in that region, he took the skin that covers the fat portion of a hog, called the leaves, and drew it over the sash tight. This furnished a very good substitute for glass; and the contrivance reflected much credit upon the inventive genius of the builder."

The cabin was furnished by Mr. Lincoln and Abraham, and we will give some account of the way of doing it.

"Bring me the auger, Abe," said his father, "and that measure, too; we must have a bedstead now."

"I can bore the holes," answered Abraham, at the same time bringing the auger and measure.

"No, you can't. It's tough work to bore two-inch

holes into such logs as these. But you can go and find me a stick for a post, and two others to lay on it."

"That all?"

"Yes, that's all. I'll just make it in that corner, and then I shall have but two holes to bore, and one post to set up. It's not more than an hour's work."

By making the bedstead in the corner, the work was but small. He measured off eight feet on one side, and bored one hole, then four and a half feet on the end, and bored another hole. Then, setting up the post in its place, two sticks from each auger hole would meet on the post, thus making the framework of the bed. This was soon done.

"Now for the bed-cord, Abe," said his father, jocosely. "We must have something to lay the bed on."

"I thought you laid on slabs," answered Abraham, not exactly comprehending the drift of his father's remark.

"We haven't any other bed-cord, so pass me some of those yonder." The slabs used to lay over the bed-frame were like those on the roof.

"How many shall I bring?" and he began to pass the slabs.

"About six, I think, will do it."

They were soon brought, and the bed was complete.

"Now, a sackful of straw on that will make a fine bed." Dry leaves, hay and husks were sometimes used for this purpose. Few had feathers in that region.

"You must keep on with your cabinet-making," said Mrs. Lincoln. "We need a table as much as a bed."

"Of course. That comes next," replied her husband. "The legs for it are all ready."

"Where are they?" inquired Abraham.

"Out there," pointing to a small pile of limbs, sticks, and slabs. Abraham went after them, while his father sawed off a puncheon of the required length for the table. A puncheon was made by splitting a log eighteen inches, more or less, in diameter, the flat side laid uppermost. Puncheons were used in this way to make tables, stools, and floors.

By the time Abraham had brought the sticks for the legs of the table, his father had the table part all ready, and was proceeding to bore the holes for the legs.

"Now you may bring some more of those sticks in the pile, — the shortest of them I shall want next."

"What for?"

"Oh, we must have some chairs now; we've sat on the ground long enough. I want the sticks for legs."

"Enough for one stool each now will do. We'll make some extra ones when we get over our hurry. Four times three are twelve; I shall want twelve."

"Must they be just alike?"

"No; you can't find two alike, hardly. If they are too long, I can saw them the right length."

All this time the work of making the table went on. As Abraham had so large a number of stool-legs to select and bring from the pile, the table was nearly completed when his part of the work was done.

"A scrumptious table, I'm thinking," said Mr. Lincoln, as he surveyed it when it was fairly on its legs. "Pioneer cabinet-work ain't handsome, but it's durable."

"And useful, too," said his wife. "Two of them wouldn't come amiss."

"No; and when I get time we'll have another. Perhaps Abe can make you one some time. Can't you make a table, Abe?"

"I can try it."

"Well, you ought to succeed, now you have seen me do it. You can try your hand at it some day. But now for the stools."

A good slab was selected, of which four stools could be made; and before night the house was furnished at small expense. A bed, table, and stools constituted the furniture of this pioneer home, in which Abraham spent twelve years of his eventful life.

Abraham occupied the loft above, ascending to his lodgings by the ladder. It was his parlor-chamber, where he slept soundly at night on the loose floor, with no other bedding than blankets. Here, year after year, he reposed nightly with as much content and bliss as we usually find in the mansions of the rich. He had never known better fare than this; and perhaps, at that age, he did not expect a larger share of worldly goods.

By this time the loss of the family by the accident on the Ohio River was nearly made good, except one or two iron kettles, and a little very poor crockery. The puncheon table and stools were replaced by better ones. Through the winter and spring, the family had got along as they could, anticipating an improved condition in the autumn.

The pioneer families of that day needed the means of converting their corn into meal. Meal was a staple article of food, without which they could scarcely survive, but there were few grist mills in all the region for many miles around. The nearest was Thompson's Ferry, where Lincoln landed on his way to Indiana. They were hand-mills, and could grind but little faster than corn could be pounded into meal with mortar and pestle.

"I'll have a mill of my own," remarked Mr. Lincoln.

"How?" inquired Abraham.

"You'll see when it is done. This going eighteen miles to mill don't pay: we must have one right here."

"And it won't take you longer to make one than it would to go to the ferry once and back," said Mrs. Lincoln.

"It's an all-day job to go there, and a pretty long day at that." She knew what kind of a mill he referred to, for she had seen them.

"We'll have one before to-morrow night," added Mr. Lincoln, with a shrug of the shoulder.

"How will you make it?" inquired Abraham, who was growing interested.

"You'll see when it's done: I shall need some of your help, and if you do first rate, you may try the rifle some day." The boy had been promised before that he should learn to shoot.

"I like that," said the lad.

"And so shall I, if you make a marksman. You can be a great help to us by killing game to cook. When you get so that you can pop over a turkey or a deer, I sha'n't need to hunt any."

"Will you let me do it?"

"Yes, and be glad to have you. The woods are full of game, and you shall have a chance to make a good shot."

Abraham was delighted with the prospect of making a gunner, and he went to his hard bed that night with glowing thoughts of the future. The morrow's sun found him up and ready to assist his father in making a grist-mill.

"The first thing is a log," said his father; and he proceeded to look for a tree of suitable dimensions; nor was he long in finding one.

"When I get it ready, I shall want you to make a fire on't, Abe," he continued.

"What! burn it up?" screamed the boy, not understanding what his father meant.

"Ha! not quite so bad as that. It wouldn't be worth much for a mill if 'twas burnt up."

"Didn't you say make a fire on it!"

"Yes, on the top of it; we must burn a hole in it a foot deep, to put corn in; so get your fire ready."

It was not long before the tree was prostrate, and a portion of the trunk cut off about four feet long. Setting it upon one end, Mr. Lincoln continued, "Here, Abe, that's what I mean by making a fire on't. You must make a fire right on the top of it, and burn a hole in it well nigh a foot deep. I'll help you."

The fire was soon kindled, and Abraham's curiosity was at the highest pitch. What was coming next was more than he could tell,— and no wonder.

"Now, bring some water; we must keep it wet."

"And put out the fire?" said Abraham, inquiringly.

"No, no; we must keep the outside of it wet, so that the whole of it won't burn. We don't want to burn the outside — only a hole in the centre."

Abraham saw through it now, and he hastened to get the water. The fire was kept burning while Mr. Lincoln looked up a spring-pole, to one end of which he attached a pestle.

"What is that for?" asked Abraham.

"You'll see when I get it into working order," replied his father. "Keep the fire a-going till it's burnt deep enough."

"It'll never burn as deep as you say."

"Yes, it will, only keep doing. That's the way pioneers have to make grist mills."

"It'll take more than one day to burn it anyhow, at this rate."

"No, it won't. It will burn faster when it gets a little deeper. We'll have it done before night. You must have patience and keep at it."

And they continued at the work. Mr. Lincoln prepared the spring-pole somewhat like an old-fashioned well-sweep; and it was ready for use before the hole was burned deep enough in the log. Then, with his additional help, the log was ready before night, and the coal was thoroughly cleaned out of the hole, and the pestle on the pole adapted thereto.

This was all the mill that he proposed to have. It was the kind used by many settlers at that day. It was a mortar and pestle on a large scale, and, on the whole, was much better than to go twenty miles to a real mill that could grind but little faster. About two quarts of corn could be put into the hole in the log at once, and a few strokes from the pestle on the spring-pole would reduce it to meal. In this way the family could be provided with meal at short notice.

The apparatus, too, corresponded very well with all the surroundings. For a Dutch oven and spider constituted the culinary furniture of the cabin. All their other articles of iron-ware were at the bottom of the Ohio River. The spider was used for griddle, stewpan, gridiron, kettle, and sundry other things, in addition to its legitimate purpose; proving that man's real wants are few in number. It is very convenient to be provided with all the modern improvements in this line; but the experience of the Lincoln family shows that happiness and life can be promoted without them.

This mill served the family an excellent purpose for several years. It was so simple that it needed no repairs, and it was not dependent either on rain or sunshine for the power to go. Any of the family could go to mill here. Abraham could carry a grist on his arm and back, and play the part of miller at the same time.

The Lincoln family was not fairly settled in Indiana until they moved into their new log-cabin in the autumn of 1817. By that time, Abraham had become a thorough pioneer boy. He had made considerable improvement, too, in "reading and writing." The impulse that Hazel gave him in Kentucky was not lost in Indiana. The three books of the family library continued to supply his intellectual wants.

During the long winter evenings of that first winter in Indiana, he read by the light of the fire; for they could not afford the luxury of any other light in their cabin. This was true, very generally, of the pioneer families: they had no more than was absolutely necessary to supply their wants. They could exist without lamp-oil or candles, and so most of them did without either. They could afford the largest fire possible, since wood was so plenty that they studied to get rid of it. Hence the light of the fire was almost equal to a good chandelier. Large logs and branches of wood were piled together in the fireplace, and its mammoth blaze lighted up every nook and corner of the dwelling. Hence lamps were scarcely needed.

He practised penmanship with a charred stick on the bark of trees and on slabs. In the winter, he wrote his name in the snow with a stick; and, in the summer, he wrote it on the ground in the garden. In this way he increased his ability to write, along with his ability to read. Still, we can scarcely conceive of a more unpromising situation for a bright boy.

The exact location of Mr. Lincoln's cabin was between the forks of Big Pigeon and Little Pigeon Creeks, one mile and a half from what is now the village of Gentryville. His cabin was surrounded with a dense forest of oaks, walnuts, sugar-maples, and other varieties of trees found in the woods of North America. The trees were of the largest growth, affording a refuge and shelter for birds and beasts, which abounded here. Deer and wild turkeys furnished abundant food for the settlers, whose experience with the rifle was their assurance of enough to eat. Lincoln was expert with the rifle, and in the forests of Indiana game met him on every hand. There was a small open space, or prairie, within a short distance from his cabin, where the deer resorted; and here he made many a good shot to supply his larder with venison.

The situation of his cabin was all that Mr. Lincoln could desire. There was one drawback, however,— there was no spring of water within a mile. One of the most fatiguing "chores" that Abraham and his sister did, in those days of hardship, was to bring water from the spring, one mile away. This need was subsequently supplied in some way. Dennis Hanks says that Mr. Lincoln "riddled his land like a honeycomb" in search of water; and, perhaps, he found it through this "riddling" process. There is a story that he employed a Yankee with a divining-rod, who directed him to excellent water for five dollars; but it is only a story.

How he obtained possession of this farm is explained by Dennis Hanks, who says, "He settled on a piece of government land,—eighty acres. The land he afterwards bought under the Two-Dollar Act; was to pay for it in instalments; one-half he paid, the other half he never paid, and finally lost the whole of the land."

We have said that Mr. Lincoln settled in Spencer County. The location of his cabin was in Perry County; but, within a few years, through increasing immigration and rapid changes and improvements, he found himself in Spencer County, with the court-house at Rockport and the village of Gentryville springing up about a mile and a half distant. Nine years after he settled in Indiana, a post-office was established at Gentryville.

David Turnham, who was a boy with Abraham in Spencer County, furnishes an interesting account of that country when he first removed thither, as follows:

"When my father came here in the spring of 1819,

he settled in Spencer County, within one mile of Thomas Lincoln, then a widower. The chance for schooling was poor; but, such as it was, Abraham and myself attended the same schools.

"We first had to go seven miles to mill; and then it was a hand-mill that would grind from ten to fifteen bushels of corn in a day. There was but little wheat grown at that time; and, when we did have wheat, we had to grind it on the mill described, and use it without bolting, as there were no bolts in the country. In the course of two or three years, a man by the name of Huffman built a mill on Anderson River, about twelve miles distant. Abe and I had to do the milling on horseback, frequently going twice to get one grist. Then they began building horse-mills of a little better quality than the hand-mills.

"The country was very rough, especially in the lowlands, so thick with bush that a man could scarcely get through on foot. These places were called Roughs. The country abounded in game, such as bears, deer, turkeys, and the smaller game.

"At that time there were a great many deer-licks; and Abe and myself would go to these licks sometimes, and watch of nights to kill deer, though Abe was not so fond of a gun as I was. There were ten or twelve of these licks in a small prairie on the creek, lying between Mr. Lincoln's and Mr. Wood's.

"The people in the first settling of this country were very sociable, kind, and accommodating; but there was more drunkenness and stealing on a small scale, more immorality, less religion, less well-placed confidence."

Mr. Turnham's allusion to the prevalence of drunkenness, at that day, renders it necessary to state that the prevalence of this evil was the source of much anxiety to Mrs. Lincoln. The danger to her boy was imminent; and many a word of warning and counsel dropped from her lips into his young ears. When Abraham began his public career, and he fearlessly and firmly avowed his total abstinence principles, he said that he owed much to one counsel of his mother; viz., "Men become drunkards because they begin to drink; if you never begin to drink, you will never become a drunkard."

The sagacity and wisdom of the mother in this striking remark will not appear to the reader until it is remembered that, at that day, there was not a total abstinence society or pledge in the world. Mrs. Lincoln had never heard of a temperance movement; for, indeed, there had been none, except on the smallest scale, in a few localities. Yet, she proposed the only safeguard to her boy, — one that proved of inestimable value to him, as he publicly and privately acknowledged many years thereafter.

We have given in detail the time, place, and circumstances of Abraham's discipline in early life, that the reader may appreciate the force of character which lifted the incubus of poverty and obscurity, and made him famous in the world.

CHAPTER V.

AFTER GAME.

T was in the spring of 1817, when Thomas Lincoln was preparing to put his first seed into the soil of Indiana, that Abraham made his first shot at game. His parents were discussing the old subject — their loss on the Ohio River; when Mrs. Lincoln remarked, —

"I'm thoroughly convinced that our loss was all for the best. I think I can see it."

"Glad if you can," replied Mr. Lincoln, "you're pretty good for seeing what nobody else can;" and he uttered this sentence rather thoughtlessly, as his mind was really absorbed in another subject.

"I don't know about that; but what in the world would you have done with all the whiskey, if we had not lost any of it in the river? Never could sell it all here, — and what a job it would have been to get it here from the Ferry!"

"Well, if I didn't sell it, we should be about as well off as we are now."

"Except the cost of getting the barrels here."

"That wouldn't be much."

"Then there's the danger of the evil it might do. It's dangerous stuff any way, as the case of many men shows."

"I know that; but I don't fear for myself."

"Neither do I fear for you; but I was thinking of Abe. You know how it is with boys in these times, and how much misery whiskey makes in a great many families. And I can't help thinking that it is all for the best that most of it is in the river."

"I can't say but what it is; I hope it is. It makes mischief enough, if that's all; and if I dreamed it would make any in my family, I should wish that all of it was at the bottom of the river."

"You may as well be glad now; for we have less to fear; and perhaps the Lord thought it was best to put so much of it where it could injure no one."

"So be it, then; but I must go to my work. This weather is too fine to be lost in doing nothing. The stuff is all sold now, so that there is no fear on that score." He sold a barrel to Posey, the teamster, who hauled his goods from the Ferry, and the remainder he disposed of in the course of the winter.

Mr. Lincoln arose and went out to his work, and within ten minutes afterwards Abraham came rushing into the cabin in a state of great excitement.

"Mother," he exclaimed, "there's a flock of turkeys right out here that I can shoot. See there," and he directed her to look through a crack in the cabin where the clay had fallen off. "Let me shoot, mother."

"Sure enough, Abe, there is a flock," responded his mother, as she caught sight of the turkeys; "a fine shot it is," and she hastened for the rifle that was always kept loaded.

"Be quick, mother, I'll fire right through the hole," continued Abe, under increasing excitement.

His mother was not long in bringing the rifle, and adjusting it through the loop-hole between the logs, when, with a few quick words of caution, she allowed him to fire.

"Bang!" went the rifle, and resounded through the forest with unusual volume, as Abraham thought in his intense earnestness. Both mother and son ran out to discover the result of the shot, and by the time they reached the spot, the smoke had cleared away, and there lay one of the flock dead.

"Killed one," shouted Abraham, as he lifted an extra large turkey from the ground.

"So you have," answered his mother, under almost as much excitement as her son.

"A monster!" continued the lad, surveying the lusty fellow with boyish pride. "Did you ever see such a big one?"

"It is a very large one," replied his mother; "that was a good shot, Abe."

By this time Mr. Lincoln had reached the spot. Hearing the report of the gun, he left his work, and hurried back to learn the cause.

"What's the firing for?" he asked hurriedly.

"I've killed a turkey," answered Abraham, exhibiting in triumph the dead bird.

"Did you do that, Abe?"

"Nobody else did it," was the boy's rather characteristic reply.

"A capital shot, Abe; you'll make a good one with the rifle if you keep on," his father added, intending to praise the boy. The fact was it was not a capital shot at all: he accidentally killed the turkey. He did not understand the use of a gun well enough to make a "capital shot." The turkey happened to sit in the way of the bullet, and was killed in consequence — that was all there was of it.

We have already said that pioneer families were dependent upon game for food. On this account fathers and sons became good marksmen, and even females were often expert with the rifle. Mrs. Lincoln could load and fire off a gun if necessary. In common with her sex, she was accustomed to such things, and adapted herself to circumstances.

Marvellous stories are told about the skill of the pioneers in the use of the rifle, and good authority substantiates their truthfulness. One writer says: "Several individuals who conceive themselves adepts in the management of the rifle, are often seen to meet for the purpose of displaying their skill; and they put up a target, in the centre of which a common-sized nail is hammered for about two-thirds its length. The marksmen make choice of what they consider a proper distance, and which may be forty paces. Each man clears the interior of his tube, places a ball in the palm of his hand, and pours as much powder from his horn as will cover it. This quantity is supposed to be sufficient for any distance short of a hundred yards. A shot that comes very close to the nail is considered that of an indifferent marksman: the bending of the nail is of course somewhat better; but nothing less than hitting it right on the head is satisfactory. One out of three shots generally hits the nail; and should the shooters amount to half a dozen, two nails are frequently needed before each can have a shot."

The same writer continues: "The snuffing of a candle with a ball I first had an opportunity of seeing near the banks of Green River, not far from a large pigeon-roost, to which I had previously made a visit. I had heard many reports of guns during the early part of a dark night, and knowing them to be those of rifles, I went forward toward the spot to ascertain the cause. On reaching the place, I was welcomed by a dozen tall, stout men, who told me they were exercising for the purpose of enabling them to shoot under night, at the reflected light from the eyes of a deer or wolf by torchlight. A fire was blazing near, the smoke of which rose curling among the thick foliage of the trees. At a distance which rendered it scarcely distinguishable, stood a burning candle, but which, in reality, was only fifty yards from the spot on which we all stood. One man was within a few yards of it to watch the effects of the shots, as well as to light the candle, should it chance to go out, or to replace it, should the shot cut it across. Each marksman shot in his turn. Some never hit either the snuff or the candle, and were congratulated with a loud laugh, while others actually snuffed the candle without putting it out, and were recompensed for their dexterity by numerous hurrahs. One of them, who was particularly expert, was very fortunate, and snuffed the candle three times out of seven, while all the other shots either put out the candle or cut it immediately under the light."

Such was the skill of riflemen at that day. Hence it was of considerable importance that boys should learn how to fire accurately. Not as a pastime was it valued, but as a means of gaining subsistence. In addition to procuring game for the table, furs were in great demand, and there were many animals valuable on this account. It was necessary, therefore, that Abraham should learn the art.

The summer of 1817 passed away, and early in the autumn the loneliness of their wilderness-life was somewhat relieved by the coming of old friends. Thomas and Betsy Sparrow, who reared Nancy Hanks (Mrs. Lincoln), came to settle by their side. Mr. Lincoln had just removed into his *new* cabin, so the Sparrows at once began housekeeping in the half-face camp. Dennis Hanks, also, had a home with the Sparrows, and Betsy was his aunt; so Dennis removed to Indiana with them.

It was a happy day for the Lincolns when the Sparrows became their neighbors. "Sparrows on the house-top," had often regaled them with song, but the human Sparrows from Kentucky were to them more than song — they were society. To Abraham especially was their coming a real godsend; for now he had an intimate and constant companion in his jolly cousin, Dennis Hanks. Such an acquisition to a boy in the woods was more of a boon than language can describe.

CHAPTER VI.

DARKER DAYS.

ABRAHAM continued to peruse the three books of the family library, — the Bible, Catechism, and Spelling-Book. There was no prospect that another book of any sort would be added to the number. The thirst for knowledge begotten in his soul already was forced to find its aliment in this narrow compass. The result was, that he knew the Spelling-Book and Catechism by heart; and he could repeat much of the Bible. His mind was hungry for knowledge; but could not find enough to eat. It was daily put upon "short allowance."

In these circumstances he longed for other books. He began to tire of the Bible. "I don't want to read the Bible all the time," he often remarked; "I wish I could have some other book to read." He did not know what other books were in existence. His parents were not wiser than he in that respect. But his mind was ravenous, and would have accepted almost any sort of a literary dish, good, bad, or indifferent. It pleaded for books.

While he was in this famishing intellectual state, a fearful disease broke out among the settlers, called "the milk disease." Cows that gave the milk, and the people who drank it, became sick, suffered, and died. The first case was fifteen or twenty miles away, but near enough to create alarm in the Lincoln cabin. It was not long, however, before the dreaded visitor came to their door. Mr. and Mrs. Sparrow were stricken down by the disease nearly at the same time. It was in the summer of 1818. Consternation now turned the attention of Abraham from books to the perils of the hour. His longing for other books was exchanged for fear of sudden death.

The Sparrows were very sick, and no doctor within thirty or forty miles. Mr. Lincoln and his wife, together with other settlers, rendered all the assistance in their power to the ill-fated couple. Week after week their sufferings were prolonged, sometimes worse, sometimes better, hope rising or waning accordingly.

"We must remove them into our cabin," said Mrs. Lincoln to her husband; "they must have better quarters and care." Mr. and Mrs. Sparrow were as father and mother to Mrs. Lincoln, and her love for them was like that of a daughter.

"Perhaps it will be best; they can't live long anywhere in my opinion," Mr. Lincoln replied.

"I can look after them much better here," continued Mrs. Lincoln; "and whether they live or die, we shall have the satisfaction of knowing that we did everything in our power for them."

The sick couple were removed into the Lincoln cabin in September, and no one was more rejoiced over the event than Dennis Hanks, to whom, also, the Sparrows were as father and mother. Dennis emphasized his joy over the removal by saying he was glad "to get out of the *mean little half-face camp.*"

The removal brought no relief to the sinking patients. In a few days both of them died, spreading gloom over the neighborhood, and creating the saddest experience Abraham and Dennis ever knew.

A spot was selected for the burial-place of the dead, about one half mile from the cabin, on a beautiful knoll that nestled under the shadow of mammoth trees. Mr. Lincoln was the only settler in the vicinity capable of making a coffin ; and he set about the sorrowful work, making them out of "green lumber, cut with a whipsaw." They were rough and heavy, like everything else connected with pioneer life ; but answered their purpose well. Without funeral ceremonies, the neighbors gathered from far and near, and tearfully committed their deceased friends to the dust.

A few days only elapsed after the burial, before Mrs. Lincoln was attacked, much more violently than the Sparrows, with the same dreaded disease. It was about three o'clock in the morning. Abraham was awakened out of a sound sleep, and hurried away for the nearest neighbor, Mrs. Woods, and, at the same time, Dennis, who became a permanent member of Lincoln's family after the death of the Sparrows, and was Abraham's bed-fellow in the loft, made his appearance, to render any assistance within his power. In the absence of physicians, a strong bond of sympathy united pioneer families, and the feminine members were always ready to tender their best nursing abilities to the sick. Nor were they altogether unsuccessful in their treatment. Some of them exhibited much skill in managing diseases, having been thrown upon their own resources for a long period, reflecting and studying for themselves. As physicians could not be had, they were compelled to do the best thing possible for themselves.

Mrs. Woods was not long in coming to her relief, and before the close of that day several other neighbors, who were notified of Mrs. Lincoln's sickness, came to proffer assistance. The tidings of her sudden attack spread so rapidly, that, within two or three days, all the pioneer families in the vicinity heard of it, and their proffers of assistance were prompt and tender. But the patient steadily grew worse, and soon became satisfied that her sickness would prove fatal. Some persons attacked with that singular disease lingered for weeks, as the Sparrows did; but Mrs. Lincoln's sickness was violent and brief. On the fifth day of October, she expired, leaving the Lincoln cabin more desolate than ever. Coming so speedily after the Sparrows passed away, death had additional terrors to the living. Dennis Hanks remembers the woe-begone appearance of Abraham from the time his mother's life was despaired of until weeks after she was laid in her grave. He was nine years old, thoughtful and sensible, not much inclined to talk about the event, but ever looking as if a pall were drawn over his heart. The reader can imagine, perhaps, what no language can convey, the loss of a good mother to a bright, obedient, and trusting boy, hid away in the woods, where a mother's presence and love must be doubly precious. The bitter experience was well suited to make the loneliness of pioneer life vastly more lonely, and its real hardships vastly harder.

Preparations were made for the burial. With his own hands, Thomas Lincoln constructed a rough coffin for his wife, and she was laid beside the Sparrows on the knoll. One party thinks that one neighbor read the Scriptures and another offered prayer; but it is probable that she was buried, as her foster-parents were, without any ceremonies — silently deposited in the ground with no special tribute, save honest tears.

Here, better than elsewhere, we can describe an event that is worthy of record. It occurred several months after the death of Mrs. Lincoln.

"You must write a letter for me, Abe, to Parson Elkins," said his father, one evening. "You can write well enough now to do that." Abraham had passed his tenth birthday.

"If you can tell me what to write, I can do it," answered the boy.

"That I will do. It will be your first letter, you know, and you must remember that your father never wrote one — never knew enough to write one."

"What do you want I should write about?" inquired Abraham.

"Write about the death of your mother. He knows nothing about it yet; and I want to ask him to visit us, and preach a funeral sermon."

"When do you want he should come?"

"When he can, I s'pose. He'll take his own time for it, though I hope he'll come soon."

"He may be dead," suggested Abraham.

"What makes you think so?"

"He's as likely to die as mother, ain't he? and he

may be dead when we don't know it, the same as she's dead when he don't know it."

"Well, there's something in that," answered his father; "but we'll see how you can make out writing a letter."

Pen and paper were provided, and Mr. Lincoln proceeded to dictate the letter. He directed him to write about the death of Mrs. Lincoln, when it occurred, and under what circumstances, and to invite him to visit them, and preach a funeral sermon. He also gave a description of their new home, and their journey thither, and wrote of their future prospects.

"Now read it over," said Mr. Lincoln.

"The whole of it?"

"Of course; I want to hear it all. I may think of something else by that time."

Abraham commenced to read it, while his father sat the very picture of satisfaction. There was genuine happiness to him in having his son prepared to write a letter. Never before had there been a member of his family who could perform this feat. It was a memorable event to him.

"See how much it is worth to be able to write," said he, as Abraham finished reading the letter. "It's worth ten times as much as it cost to be able to write only that one letter."

"It ain't much work to learn to write," said Abraham; "I'd work as hard again for it before I'd give it up."

"You'd have to give it up, if you were knocked about as I was when a boy."

"I know that."

"You don't know it as I do; and I hope you never will. But it's worth more than the best farm to know how to write a letter as well as that."

"I shall write one better than that yet," said Abraham. "But how long will it take for the letter to go to Parson Elkins?"

"That's more than I can tell; but it will go there some time, and I hope it will bring him here."

"He won't want to come so far as this," suggested Abraham.

"It ain't so far for him as it was for us."

"Why ain't it?"

"Because he lives nearer the line of Indiana than we did. It ain't more than seventy-five miles for him to come, and he often rides as far as that."

The letter went on its errand, and Abraham was impatient to learn the result. On the whole, it was rather an important event in his young life, — the writing of that first letter. Was it strange that he should query whether it would reach the good minister to whom it was sent? Would it be strange if the writing of it proved one of the happy influences that started him off upon a career of usefulness and fame? We shall see.

Mr. Lincoln had much to say to his neighbors about the letter that his son had written, and they had much to say to him. It was considered remarkable for a boy of his age to do such a thing. Not one quarter of the adults in all that region could write; and this fact rendered the ability of the boy in this regard all the more marvellous. It was noised abroad, and the result was, that Abraham had frequent applications from the neighbors to write letters for them. Nor was he indisposed to gratify their wishes. One of his traits of character was a generous disposition to assist others, and it prompted him to yield to their wishes in writing letters for them. Nor was it burdensome to him, but the opposite. He delighted to do it. And thus, as a consequence of his acquiring the art of penmanship, far-distant and long-absent friends of the pioneer families heard from their loved ones.

The letter brought the parson. After the lapse of about three months he came. The letter reached him in Kentucky, after considerable delay, and he embraced the first opportunity to visit his old friends. Abraham had almost concluded that his letter was lost, as the favorite minister did not come. But one day, when the lad was about two miles from home, who should he see coming but Parson Elkins, on his old bay horse! He recognized him at once, and was delighted to see him.

"Why, Abe, is that you?" exclaimed the parson. "Am I so near your home?"

"Yes, sir; did you get my letter?" Abraham thought of the memorable letter the first thing. He had good evidence before him that the letter reached its destination, but he would know certainly.

"Your letter!" exclaimed Parson Elkins, inquiringly. "I got your father's letter." Abraham did not stop to think that the letter went in his father's name.

"I wrote it," he said.

"*You* wrote it! Is that so?"

"Yes, sir; father can't write, you know."

"O, yes; I do remember now that he couldn't write;

and so you did it? Not many boys that can write like that."

"It was the first letter I ever wrote."

"Better still is that,—the first one? Well, you needn't be ashamed of that."

They were advancing towards the cabin during this conversation, Abraham running alongside the horse, and the parson looking kindly upon him.

"There's our house!" exclaimed Abraham, as they came in sight of it. "We live there," pointing with his finger.

"Ah! that's a pleasant place to live. And there's your father, I think, too."

"Yes, that's he. He'll be glad to see you."

"And I shall be glad to see him."

By this time they came near Mr. Lincoln, who recognized Parson Elkins, and gave him a most cordial greeting. He was really taken by surprise, although he had not relinquished all expectation of the parson coming.

"You find me in a lonely condition," said Mr. Lincoln. "Death has made a great change in my family."

"Very great indeed," responded Mr. Elkins. "I know how great your loss is; but 'Whom the Lord loveth, he chasteneth.'"

Assenting to this, Mr. Lincoln continued,—

"Now, let me say, that, while you are here, I want you should preach a funeral sermon. You know all about my wife. You will stay over next Sunday, won't you?" It was now Wednesday.

"Why, yes, I can stay as long as that, though I must be about my Master's work."

"You will be about your Master's work, if you stay and preach a funeral sermon; and it may do a great sight of good."

"Very true; and I shall be glad to stay; for if any one ever deserved a funeral sermon, it is your wife. But where shall I preach it?"

"At her grave. I've had that arranged in my mind for a long time; and we'll notify the people; there will be a large attendance. The people thought a deal of her here."

It was arranged that Mr. Elkins should preach the funeral sermon at the grave of Mrs. Lincoln on the following Sabbath. Accordingly, notice was sent abroad to the distance of twelve or fifteen miles, and a platform was erected near the grave. Every preparation was made for the solemn event. Although nearly a year had elapsed since Mrs. Lincoln died, yet a sermon to her memory was no less interesting to her surviving friends.

In the mean time, Mr. Elkins busied himself in intercourse with the family; and he visited some of the neighbors, and conversed with them on spiritual things. Abraham, too, received his special attention. The boy had improved rapidly since he left Kentucky, and his remarkable precocity was suited to draw the attention of such a preacher.

The Sabbath arrived, — a bright, beautiful day. From a distance of twelve or fifteen miles, the settlers came to listen to the sermon. Entire families assembled, parents and children, from the oldest to the youngest. Hoary age and helpless childhood were there. They came in carts, on horseback, and on foot, any way to get there. As they had preaching only when one of these pioneer preachers visited that vicinity, it was a treat to most of the inhabitants, and they manifested their interest by a general turn-out. The present occasion, however, was an unusual one, as the funeral sermon of Mrs. Lincoln was to be preached.

Parson Elkins was an earnest man, and the occasion inspired him with unusual fervor. None of the people had ever listened to him before, except the Lincoln family, and they were delighted with his services. His tribute to the memory of Mrs. Lincoln was considered just and excellent. None thought that too much was said in her praise. On the other hand, the general feeling was rather, as one of the number expressed it, that, "say what he might in praise of her, he couldn't say too much."

Abraham was deeply interested in the sermon, and it brought all his mother's tenderness and love afresh to his mind. To him it was almost like attending her funeral over again. Her silent dust was within a few feet of him, and vivid recollection of her worth was in his heart.

He drank in the sentiments of the discourse, too. He usually did this, as he was accustomed to think for himself. A few years later he often criticized the sermons to which he listened, much to the amusement of those with whom he conversed. He sometimes called in question the doctrines preached. This was one of the things in which his precocity appeared. It was at this point that his mental activity and power were often seen. But the sentiments of the aforesaid funeral sermon especially impressed his mind.

At this time of his life he was a close listener to the conversation of the neighbors; and he would become almost vexed over the conversation of some of them, who talked so unintelligibly through ignorance, that he could not understand them. His active brain labored to compass every subject, and he sometimes fretted over unlettered talkers whose meaning he failed to comprehend. After he came into the possession of additional books, he was wont to discuss their subject-matter, and express his own views freely.

In this respect he was unlike most boys, who are superficial in their views of things. They read, and that is the end of it. They think no more about it, — at least, they do not inquire into the *why* and *wherefore* of matters stated; and so the habit of sliding over things loosely is formed. They do not think for themselves. They accept things as true, because others say they are true. They are satisfied with knowing that things *are*, without asking *why* they are. But Abraham was not so. He thought, reflected; and this developed his mental powers faster than even school could do it.

The reader should understand more about these pioneer preachers, in order to appreciate the influences that formed Abraham's character, and therefore we will stop here to give some account of them.

They were not generally men of learning and culture, though some of them were men of talents. Few, if any of them, were ever in college, and some of them were never in school. But they had a call to preach, as they believed, and good and true hearts for doing it. Many of them preached almost every day, travelling from place to place on horseback, studying their sermons in the saddle, and carrying about with them all the library they had in their saddle-bags. They stopped where night overtook them, and it was sometimes miles away from any human habitation, with no bed but the earth, and no covering but the canopy of heaven. They labored without a salary, and were often poorly clothed and scantily fed, being constrained to preach by the love of Christ. The following account of two pioneer preachers, by Milburn, will give the reader a better idea of this class of useful men than any description of ours, and it will be read with interest : —

" One of these preachers, who travelled all through the Northwestern Territory, a tall, slender, graceful man, with a winning countenance and kindly eye, greatly beloved by all to whom he ministered, was presented by a large landholder with a title-deed of three hundred and twenty acres. The preacher was extremely poor, and there had been many times when he received scarcely enough support to keep soul and body together. Yet he labored on, and did much good. He seemed pleased with his present of land, and went on his way with a grateful heart. But in three months he returned, and met his benefactor at the door, saying, ' Here, sir, I want to give you back your title-deed.'

"' What's the matter?' said his friend, surprised. ' Any flaw in it ?'

" ' No.'

" ' Isn't it good land ?'

" ' Good as any in the State.'

"'Sickly situation?'

"'Healthy as any other.'

"'Do you think I repent my gift?'

"'I haven't the slightest reason to doubt your generosity.'

"'Why don't you keep it, then?'

"'Well, sir,' said the preacher, 'you know I am very fond of singing, and there's one hymn in my book the singing of which is one of the greatest comforts of my life. I have not been able to sing it with my whole heart since I was here. A part of it runs in this way:—

> "No foot of land do I possess
> No cottage in the wilderness;
> A poor wayfaring man,
> I lodge awhile in tents below,
> And gladly wander to and fro,
> Till I my Canaan gain;
> There is my house and portion fair,
> My treasure and my heart are there,
> And my abiding home."

"'Take your title-deed,' he added; 'I had rather sing that hymn with a clear conscience than own America.'

"There was another preacher of the pioneer class so intent upon his work that hunger and nakedness did not affright him. He was more scholarly than most of the preachers around him, and often sat up half the night, at the cabins of the hunters where he stopped, to study. These cabins were about twelve by fourteen feet, and furnished accommodations for the family, sometimes numbering ten or twelve children; and, as the forests abounded in '*varmints*,' the hens and chickens were taken in for safe keeping. Here, after the family had retired, he would light a pine knot, 'stick it up in one corner of the huge fireplace, lay himself down on the flat of his stomach in the ashes,' and study till far into the night.

"Many a time was the bare, bleak mountain-side his bed, the wolves yelling a horrid chorus in his ears. Sometimes he was fortunate enough to find a hollow log, within whose cavity he inserted his body, and found it a good protection from the rain or frost.

"Once, seated at the puncheon dinner-table with a hunter's family, the party is startled by affrighted screams from the door-yard. Rushing out, they behold a great wildcat bearing off the youngest child. Seizing a rifle from the pegs over the door, the preacher raises it to his shoulder, casts a rapid glance along the barrel, and delivers his fire. The aim has been unerring, but too late,— the child is dead, already destroyed by the fierce animal.

"That same year he had a hand-to-hand fight with a bear, from which conflict he came forth victor, his knife entering the vitals of the creature just as he was about to be enfolded in the fatal hug.

"Often he emerged from the wintry stream, his garments glittering in the clear, cold sunlight, as if they had been of burnished steel armor, chill as the touch of death. During that twelvemonth, in the midst of such scenes, he travelled on foot and horseback *four thousand miles, preached four hundred times*, and found, on casting up the receipts,— yarn socks, woollen vests, cotton shirts, and a little silver change,

—that his salary amounted to *twelve dollars and ten cents.*

"Yet he persevered, grew in knowledge and influence, became a doctor of divinity, and finally was made president of a university. He is known on the page of history as Henry Bidleman Bascom."

Such were the pioneer preachers of the West; of simple-hearted piety, lofty faith, a fiery zeal, unwavering fortitude, and a practical turn of mind, through which they did a great work for God.

We have made this digression from the thread of our story, to show what influences of the ministry were thrown around Abraham's early life. It is true the preachers to whom he listened were not "circuit-riders," as travelling preachers were called. They were Baptist ministers, who lived within twenty miles, and who occasionally preached in that neighborhood. During the first few years of Abraham's residence in Indiana, there was one Jeremiah Cash, who sometimes preached in the vicinity, and the young listener became much interested in him. A few years later, two others came to that section of country to live. Their names were John Richardson and Young Lamar. One of them dwelt seven or eight miles from Abraham's home on the north, and the other eight or ten miles to the south; and both of them were wont to preach at Mr. Lincoln's cabin, and at other cabins, as they had opportunity. Sometimes they preached in the open air, as Mr. Elkins did the funeral sermon. This was always the case when more people attended than could crowd into a log-house.

Such was all the pulpit influence that reached the boyhood and youth of Abraham. Yet it left indelible impressions upon his mind. Though it was small and inconstant, apparently, in comparison with the pulpit advantages that boys enjoy at the present day, it imbued his soul with sentiments that were never obliterated. He was much indebted to the unpolished eloquence of those pioneer preachers, whose sterling piety caused them to proclaim the truth with fidelity and earnestness. This was one of the few influences that contributed to make him a remarkable man.

CHAPTER VII.

BRIGHTER HOURS.

ABRAHAM deeply felt the change that death had wrought in his cabin home, and, for weeks, his mind was absorbed in his loss. Perhaps his oppressive sense of loneliness and his grief would have continued, but for an unexpected blessing that came to him in the shape of a book. His father met with a copy of The Pilgrim's Progress, at the house of an acquaintance, twenty miles away or more, and he borrowed it for Abraham. The boy was never more happily surprised than he was when his father, on his return, said:

"Look here, Abe, I've found something for you," at the same time exhibiting the book.

"Found it!" exclaimed Abraham, supposing that his father meant that he picked it up in the woods or fields.

"No, no; you don't understand me. I meant that I came across it at Pierson's house, and I borrowed it for you."

"Pilgrim's Progress," said Abraham, taking the book and reading the title; "that will be good, I should think." He knew nothing about the book; he never heard of it before.

"I shall want to hear it," said his father. "I heard about that book many years ago, but I never heard it read."

"What is it about?" asked Abraham.

"You'll find that out by reading it," answered his father.

"And I won't be long about it neither," continued Abraham. "I know I shall like it."

"I know you will, too."

"I don't see how you know, if you never heard it read."

"On account of what I've heard about it."

And it turned out to be so. Abraham sat down to read the volume very much as some other boys would sit down to a good dinner. He found it better even than he expected. It was the first volume that he was provided with after the spelling-book, Catechism, and Bible, and a better one could not have been found. He read it through once, and was half-way through it a second time, when he received a present of another volume, in which he became deeply interested. It was Æsop's Fables, presented to him, partly on account of his love of books, and partly because it would serve to occupy his mind and lighten his sorrow.

He read the fables over and over until he could repeat almost the entire contents of the volume. He was thoroughly interested in the moral lesson that each fable taught, and derived therefrom many valuable hints that he carried with him through life. On the whole, he spent more time over Æsop's Fables than he did over The Pilgrim's Progress, although he was really charmed by the latter. But there was a practical turn to the fables that interested him, and he could easily recollect the stories. Perhaps his early familiarity with this book laid the foundation for that facility at apt story-telling that distinguished him through life. It is easy to see how such a volume might beget and foster a taste in this direction. Single volumes have moulded the reader's character and decided his destiny more than once, and that, too, when far less absorbing interest was manifested in the book. It is probable, then, that Æsop's Fables exerted a decided influence upon Abraham's character and life. The fact that he read the volume so much as to commit the larger part of it to memory adds force to this opinion.

With two new books of such absorbing interest, it was not strange that Abraham was disposed to neglect his daily labor. His father could readily discover that Æsop had more attractions for him than ax or hoe. Nor was he inclined to break the spell that bound him until he actually feared that the books would make him "lazy."

"Come, Abe, you mustn't neglect your work; we've lots to do, and books must not interfere," was his father's gentle rebuke.

"In a minute," answered the boy, just like most other boys of that age, who are "book-worms."

"That's what makes boys lazy, waiting to play or read, when they ought to be at work," continued his father. "All study and no work is 'most as bad as all work and no study."

"Only a minute, and I'll go," added Abraham, so absorbed in his book that he scarcely knew what answer he made.

"It must be a short minute," retorted his father in a tone of injured authority.

"I'll work hard enough to make it up when I get at it," said Abraham, still delaying.

"I don't know about that. I'm afraid that your thoughts will be somewhere else; so put down the book and come on."

With evident reluctance the young reader laid down his book, preliminary to obeying orders.

"Good boys obey at once," continued his father; "don't have to drive 'em like cattle."

"I only wanted to read a minute longer," answered Abraham, by way of palliating his offence.

"And I only wanted you shouldn't," exclaimed his father angrily. "I know what is best for you. I'm willing you should read and write, but you must work when work drives."

It was altogether new for Abraham to exhibit so much disobedience as he did after he became enthusiastic over The Pilgrim's Progress and Æsop's Fables. Nor was he conscious of possessing a disobedient spirit; for no such spirit was in his heart. He was simply infatuated with the new books.

We must not conceal the fact that his father had been somewhat annoyed by the boy's method of improving his penmanship by writing with chalk or a charred stick upon almost any surface that came in his way. But for his paternal pride over this acquisition of his boy, he might have checked him in this singular way of improvement. One incident occurred that served to reconcile his father in the main to his scrawls here and there, although he may have thought still that Abraham was carrying the matter too far.

An acquaintance came into the field where father and son were at work, when his eye was arrested by letters cut in the mellow soil.

"What's that?" he inquired.

Abraham smiled, and let his father answer.

"What's what?"

"Why, this writing, — it looks as if somebody had been writing on the ground."

"Abe's work, I s'pose."

"Abe didn't do that!" answered the neighbor.

"I did do it with a stick," said the boy.

"What is it?" The man couldn't read.

"It's my name."

"Your name, hey? Likely story."

"Well, 'tis, whether you believe it or not;" and he proceeded to spell it out, — "A-B-R-A-H-A-M L-I-N-C-O-L-N."

"Sure enough, it is; and you certainly did it, Abe?"

"Yes, sir; and I will do it again, if you want to see me;" and, without waiting for an answer, he caught up a stick, and wrote his name again in the dirt.

"There 'tis," said Abraham.

"I see it, and it's well done," answered the neighbor.

And there, on the soil of Indiana, Abraham Lincoln wrote his name, with a stick, in large characters, — a sort of prophetic act, that students of history may love to ponder. For, since that day, he has written his name, by public acts, on the annals of every State in the Union.

From the time, however, that Abraham became absorbed in The Pilgrim's Progress and Æsop's Fables, he was subject to the charge of being "lazy." The charge gained force, too, as he grew older, and more books and increasing thirst for knowledge controlled him. Dennis Hanks said: "Abe was lazy, very lazy. He was always reading, scribbling, ciphering, writing poetry, and such like." John Romine declared that "Abe was awful lazy. He worked for me; was always reading and thinking; I used to get mad at him. He worked for me pulling fodder. I say Abe was awful lazy. He would laugh and talk, and crack jokes, and tell stories all the time; didn't love work, but did dearly love his pay. He worked for me frequently, a few days only at a time. He said to me one day, that his father taught him to work, but never learned him to love it."

Mrs. Crawford, for whose husband Abraham worked, and in whose cabin he read and told stories, said: "Abe was no hand to pitch into work like killing snakes." At the same time, Mr. Crawford could find no man to suit him as well as Abraham, when the latter was but fifteen years of age.

We protest, here and now, against this charge of laziness which some biographers have made so prominent. Nothing was ever more common than to charge studious boys and girls with laziness. A great many men and women, who know no better, bring the same charge against professional gentlemen. Any person who is not obliged to work on the farm, or at the forge, or engage in some other manual labor, for a livelihood, they pronounce lazy and aristocratic. Through sheer ignorance, studying and literary aspirations are regarded as proof of laziness. It was so in Abraham's time. Because he possessed talents that craved knowledge as the appetite craves food, leading him to snatch fragments of time for reading, and perhaps to devote hours to the bewitching pastime that ought to have been given to hard work, careless, ignorant observers called him "lazy." It is a base slander. There was not a lazy bone in him. The boy who will improve such bits of time as he can save from his daily toil for study, and sit up nights to read the Life of Washington, or master a problem in mathematics, is not lazy. He may love a book more than he loves chopping or threshing, just as another may love the latter more than he does the former; but he is not lazy. Laziness wastes the spare hours of the day in bringing nothing to pass, and gives the night to sleep instead of mental improvement. As many of the busiest and most cheerful workers in our country are its scholars, without a particle of the element of laziness in their composition, so many of the most industrious and noble boys are those who prefer a book to the plow, and would rather go to school than to harvesting. That was true of Abraham Lincoln. His heart was set on books; but his hands were so ready for hard work, that any farmer was glad to hire him at the age of fourteen or fifteen years of age, because he would do more work than any youth of his age. He would chop more wood in a day, lift larger logs, and "pull more fodder," boy as he was, than half the men who hired him.

True, from the time that John Baldwin, the blacksmith, came into the neighborhood, when Abraham was about ten years old, he would steal away to the smithy's shop to listen to his stories. John was a great story-teller, and he was fond of children also, and these were attractions enough for such a precocious boy. His mind yearned for thoughts; it was desperate for entertainment; and the blacksmith's stories, and incidents of his life, supplied both thoughts and entertainment. He spent much time with this jolly son of Vulcan before he began to tell stories himself, and, after that, he exchanged them with the smutty toiler at the forge. But there was no evidence of laziness in those visits to the blacksmith's shop. And when we place this freak of a singularly bright boy, together with all his other acts that denoted laziness to the ignorant pioneers, beside the fact, that in manhood, to the day of his death, Abraham Lincoln was one of the hardest workers who ever lived, both at manual and intellectual labor, ignoring all ten hour systems, and toiling fifteen, sixteen, and even eighteen hours a day, to satisfy his honorable ambition, the charge of laziness is branded as slander on the part of those who make it. "The boy is father to the man,"—the lazy boy makes the lazy man, and *vice versa*. If Abraham was a lazy boy, his manhood completely belied his youth, and the old maxim is exploded.

We have seen that they who called him lazy coupled the charge with the statement that he was always "reading and thinking," evidently considering that his love of books was proof of a disposition to shirk labor. Their ignorance is the explanation of, and excuse for, their charge.

We have made this digression, at this point, in order to direct the attention of the reader to an important element of Lincoln's character, that will find ample support in the sequel.

Now that we are speaking of Abraham's books, we may record the facts about two other volumes, that came into his hands within two years after Æsop's Fables. They were Ramsay's Life of Washington, and Robinson Crusoe.

Dennis Hanks came home one day and said to Abraham, —

"Don't you want to read the life of Washington?"

"Of course I do," was his reply. "What do you ask me that for?"

"Because I've seen one."

"Where?"

"Down at Anderson's Creek."

"Whom did it belong to?"

Dennis told him, adding, "He offered to lend it to me."

"Then *I* can borrow it?"

"Any time you are there; there's no doubt of it."

Without recording the details of this affair, it will answer our purpose to say that Abraham embraced the first opportunity to secure the loan of that valuable biography. He knew that Washington was called the "father of his country"—that he was commander-in-chief of the army in the American Revolution. He had been told, also, of the part his grandfather took in the "war of independence." This was all he knew of the illustrious statesman whose life he purposed to read; but this was quite enough to awaken his enthusiasm over the volume. It was read and re-read with the deepest interest, and its contents discussed with his father and Dennis, both of whom learned more about Washington and his times from Abraham than they ever knew before.

It is not known how he came into possession of Robinson Crusoe. Doubtless the book was borrowed; and it proved a source of genuine satisfaction to him. Once reading it only created the desire to read it a second time, and even a third time. There was a kind of witchery about the book to his active mind, different from that exerted over him even by The Pilgrim's Progress. He could scarcely command language to express his admiration of the volume.

www.ingramcontent.com/pod-product-compliance
Lightning Source LLC
Chambersburg PA
CBHW020330090426
42735CB00009B/1482